From the Author

The contents of this book are intended to stimulate the wealth of imagination in children (and parents too). Here is an assortment of things that children would love to build, all within their average abilities and ambitions.

By presenting a clear picture of each project, without detailed and complicated plans, the child is respondent to his or her own resourcefulness and imagination. It is not the author's intention that each finished project be exactly like the drawing, but only that the pictorial concept will inspire a constructive effort toward these or any other things that are fun to build.

Adults should inspect and approve the building efforts of children under their supervision and are encouraged to participate in the construction of these projects as well.

By employing common sense and a safety-first attitude, all builders inspired by this book can enjoy many hours of outdoor fun and memorable play. Happy building!

Special Thanks To:

Copy editors
Gary L. Armstrong
Christy Gustaitis-Ritner, B.A., M.A.,
La Habra, CA

Additional graphic design
Bob Payne Design, Garden Grove, CA

A BARREL OF FUN WITH BOXES AND BOARDS AN

"Backyard" THINGS
THAT ARE FUN TO BUILD!

by Ray Wallace

"Backyard" Things That Are Fun To Build!
by Raymond E. Wallace

Copyright © 1996 by Raymond E. Wallace

First Printing 1996

Published by:

Infotainment

P.O. Box 1244
Parker, Colorado 80134-1244 U.S.A.

Publisher's Cataloging in Publication
(Prepared by Quality Books Inc.)

Wallace, Raymond E.
    Backyard things that are fun to build! / by Ray Wallace.
    p. cm.
    SUMMARY: Eighteen how-to building projects for children, completely illustrated with general construction guidelines, featuring forts and other realistic playthings constructed from common scrap material and recycled household items.
    ISBN 0-9651275-6-7

    1. Toy making--Juvenile literature. 2. Handicraft--Juvenile literature. 3. Recycling (Waste, etc.)--Juvenile literature. I. Title.

TT174.W35 1996   745.592
                                QBI96-20165

LCCN#: 96-75668

Printed and bound in Hong Kong

Dedicated to Jimmie and Robbie

...PES AND CANS AND CARTONS AND NAILS AND WHEELS

About the Author

Ray Wallace has loved to build and draw ever since he was a child. Raised in Corona Del Mar, California, Ray spent many happy hours dreaming up and building "backyard things" with his neighborhood buddies. Inexpensive, educational and pure fun, these scrap-lumber creations became one of his passions.

Through this early creative play, Ray developed many practical skills which served him well later in life. As a teenager, Ray became the first boy scout in the United States to achieve eagle scout twice (eagle scout and quarter master). As a reward, Ray was selected for a "hunting excursion" across the South Seas in the expedition ship Stranger. It was 1934, and World War II was on the horizon. To Ray's surprise, he discovered the "excursion" was secretly charting the South Seas in preparation for conflict!

Eventually, Ray put his drawing skills to work as staff artist for the Copley newspaper chain. After establishing his own advertising agency, Ray needed a "keep-busy" project between jobs. He began to sketch all the wonderful backyard things he had loved and made as a youngster. The result is the one-of-a-kind book you now hold in your hands, *"Backyard" Things That Are Fun To Build!*

Over the years, Ray has continued to design and build. One of his many designs for the amusement industry is the Columbia Sailing Ship located in the Rivers of America at Disneyland®. In fact, Ray was designated honorary captain of the Columbia by Walt Disney in 1958.

Today, Ray Wallace, renowned designer, artist, architect, licensed master mariner and ocean-racing yachtsman, is founder and C.E.O. of Special Productions, Inc. in San Pedro, California, a world leader in design, architecture and construction for amusement park and recreation industries. Ray's international roster of clients includes: Six Flags®, Sea World®, Knott's Berry Farm®, The Walt Disney Company® and many more. A reputable award-winning artist, specializing in representational fine art, Ray Wallace is unique in his comprehension of art and architecture and its influential effect on people.

From the Publishers

As young boys, we received *"Backyard" Things That Are Fun To Build!* as a Christmas gift from our father, Norman Armstrong. It was an instant hit! We grew up with the book, making "backyard things" that, like Ray's experience, became one of our creative passions. Today, we are the proud owners and operators of Infotainment, blending information and entertainment into unique educational resources for children. We specialize in fun. Along with Ray Wallace, we are honored to bring you this finely crafted, completely unique and inspired book. Enjoy!

Gary L. Armstrong   *Wayne Armstrong*

Table of Contents

Train Engine

Here's a real fun thing to make — a steam engine and car to carry supplies, gold and passengers from the seaport to the fort!

Guess we'll need another wagon to build this one or maybe two wagons if you want a coal car. If you or your friends don't have a wagon, you can make one like the chassis of the Hot Rod Car on page 27. This can be a convertible wagon to use for lots of fun projects in this book.

Next, you should look for a big round barrel, metal drum, cracker box or anything round like a big can for the engine boiler. Then find some fairly large wooden boxes or packing crates. If you take the side off one of the boxes, and extend the top up high with some boards or sticks, you have the engine cab. Another box, or maybe two boxes will make the coal or wood box and the seat for passengers or army supplies.

A big coffee or juice can makes a fine smoke stack, and an upside down pan or pot can look just like a real sand dome. Another big coffee can or round oatmeal box will make a good steam cylinder. Bet you can think of a lot more things to put on your engine to make it look real.

Fixing up the inside of the cab is even more fun. A real set of brakes that you can work inside the cab is easy to make and will help you stop when you need to. If you can find a bunch of pipes or a hose and dials and things, you can hook them all up to look like a real engine cab. An old faucet or a water valve would make a good throttle.

After you make your engine real good, you can make it look even better by painting it. Checkout a library book on steam trains to see what colors your locomotive should be.

It's a lot of fun to build other things for your backyard railroad too. You could make signals, crossing gates and a real passenger or freight station. If you can get some other wagons, you could make more cars, then you could charge maybe a dime to carry passengers around the block.

3

Covered Wagon

Just like the pioneers, you could build a whole bunch of covered wagons and have a real wagon train. When your camp gets attacked, you could form all the wagons in a big circle and have a real cap gun battle. Covered wagons are fun and real easy to build.

First, you or one of your friends have to get a wagon. Then you go to the back of a store and ask for two wooden boxes, a big one and a little one. When you find some sticks that bend, arch them over and nail the ends inside the big box, like in the picture. Ask mom or dad for an old sheet or some cloth. Then hang the cloth on the bent sticks and tuck it around the sticks on the front and back end. Maybe you can tack the sides down to the box. The little box goes in front of the big box for a seat for the driver. Some boards can be propped up in front or nailed to the little box for the driver's feet. If you want, you can put a brake on as it shows in the picture. Maybe mom or dad can help you make this work real well.

Oatmeal boxes, ice cream cartons or big cans make good water barrels for the side. A good idea is to put an old shovel on the side, too, and then, you can dig out of real sandy places. If you tie a round piece of wood to the wagon handle, you and a friend can pull it easier. If the box is pretty big, you could pull three passengers and a dog around and maybe go down the street and blaze a trail across a big lot to discover gold. Let's see if you can figure out how to make the box stay on the wagon. It's easy if you just think about it.

4

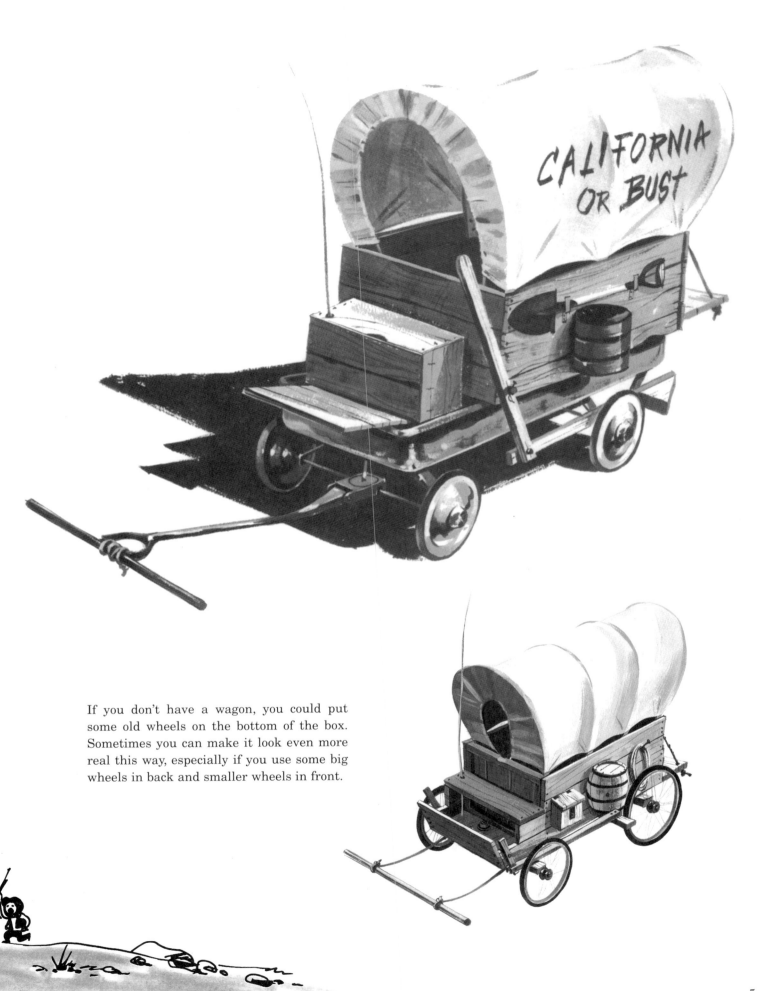

If you don't have a wagon, you could put some old wheels on the bottom of the box. Sometimes you can make it look even more real this way, especially if you use some big wheels in back and smaller wheels in front.

Twin Jet *DELTA WING INTERCEPTOR*

with controls that really work

First there's the whine of the starter, then a deafening roar and finally as your jet interceptor races down the runway, the big jet engines make a whistling roar, and you're off the ground, landing gear up and locked, streaking into the sky after an enemy bomber.

For all of this fun you can build the super jet interceptor and be the best airplane builder and jet pilot in the neighborhood.

A large wooden box for the main fuselage and pilot's cockpit will get you started. Then you build a triangle-shaped framework around the box as it shows in the picture. If you cover this with cardboard and paint it with insignias, it will look like a real delta wing.

The two jet engines can be made from some old stovepipe or heavy cardboard rug cores from a store where they sell carpeting. Or maybe you can make them by bending light cardboard in a tube shape. The tail can be made with a long board like the picture shows. It's fun to see if you can fix the controls so that they will move the hinged control surfaces (ailerons) in the ends of the wings and the tail (elevator and rudder). You will need some wire, string or rope for this.

In the cockpit you should have a joystick and a rudder bar. When you push the joystick forward the tail "elevator" should go down. If you pull it back, the "elevator" should go up. When you push the stick to the right, the right "aileron" should go up and the left "aileron" should go down. If you push the stick to the left, just the opposite should happen. The rudder bar should be a board with a nail or bolt through the center so your feet can make it turn. Wires or strings should go from the ends of the rudder bar right back to the control "horns" on the rudder. When you push the rudder bar with your right foot, the rudder should turn to the right.

This is another project where you can have fun fixing up the cockpit with all kinds of dials and switches. Some pipes sticking out of the wings could be machine guns too. Remember the trigger for the guns is always in the grip-handle of the joystick.

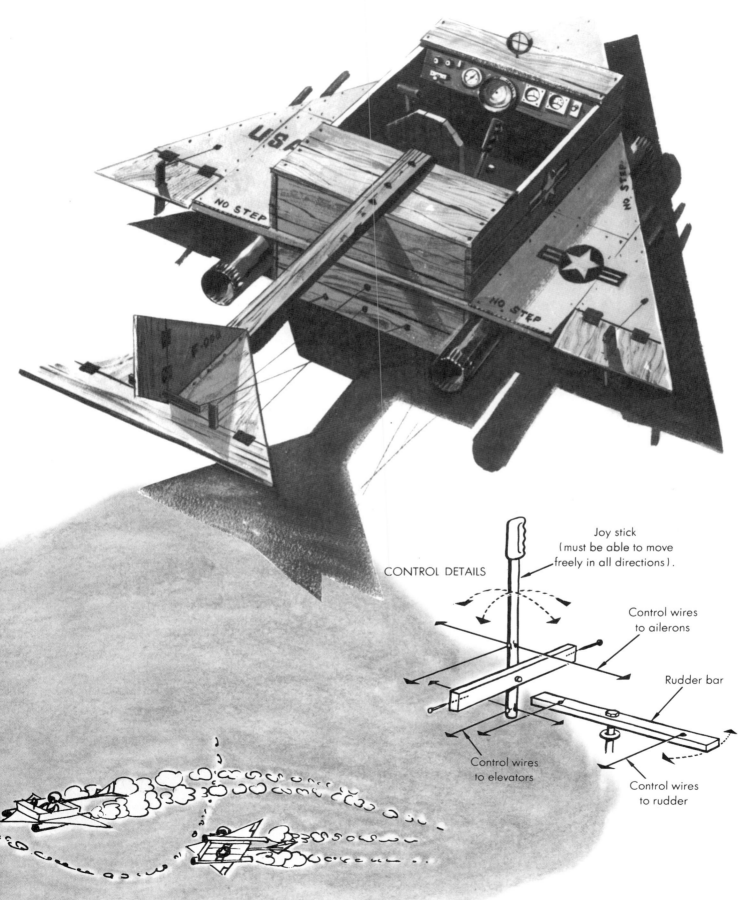

CONTROL DETAILS

Joy stick
(must be able to move
freely in all directions).

Control wires
to ailerons

Rudder bar

Control wires
to elevators

Control wires
to rudder

Frontier Fort

Think of all the fun you'd have with a real frontier fort. Here's where your troops can camp overnight or plan patrols and wilderness expeditions. Maybe you could build a tepee village right near the fort and trade with the neighborhood tribe.

Next time you are near a place where they sell bicycles, ask the salesperson for some bicycle cartons or boxes. These are big and sort of flat and easy to cut to make walls and doors. Be very careful when you are cutting cardboard and always push the knife away from you. Remember, when building, always think safety first.

Get some posts and stick them in the ground where your fort is going to be. You may have to dig a hole first. Then nail some long strips of wood across the top and bottom of the posts, but leave an opening where you want the gate. When you have cut the cardboard, nail the big pieces on the outside of the wooden strips, then you will have walls for your fort. If you want, you can cut the top edge of the cardboard to look like sharpened posts, like in the picture. The gates can be two pieces of cardboard nailed to the gate posts. You don't need hinges because the cardboard will bend.

You should make the walls about as high as your head or maybe a little higher. If you have room in your backyard or in a vacant lot, you can make it pretty big, but you should get some friends to help you.

Maybe you can find some more lumber and boxes and sawhorses, and build a general's headquarters and ramparts to shoot toy guns from. A cot under the ramparts makes a good hospital.

A good idea is to make the gate big enough to get the covered wagon or stage coach inside, so you can save the settlers from outside attacks.

Pirate Ship

Here is a real full-size pirate ship that can be more fun than anything! Like the real old treasure galleons of long ago, it has a sail that really works, a poop deck, cannons, anchors and a roomy cabin for the pirate captain.

It's sort of a big project, but if you can get mom, dad or some friends to help, you could make it in a couple of weekends. By looking closely at the picture and some of the directions you can write down the things you'll need to build it with. Be sure to study all the pictures, so you can see how the parts go together. Also, make sure everything is safe, strong and secure before playing on it.

Maybe you can think of some other things besides the stuff in the directions. For instance, the masts and yards don't have to be round. They could be long pieces of lumber such as posts or two-by-fours. Old dead tree trunks and limbs, even old lengths of pipe will make good spars.

The pirate ship pictured is about six feet wide. That's about as wide as the door of a house is tall. It should be about 15 or 20 feet long. Maybe you would rather make a smaller one. Even if you make a little one, a pirate ship flying the Jolly Roger flag will be great fun for you and your friends.

When you are a little older and want to join the Sea Scouts or Sea Explorers, you and your shipmates can build an even bigger ship like this for your Sea Scout meetings or training. If you are a good swimmer and live near the water, you could build a big raft, then build the ship on top of it, then you'd have a real floating pirate ship. But land ships are a lot of fun too.

(Small parts instructions)

1. **ANCHOR** You can make a great anchor out of sticks about one inch thick and two inches wide. Just cut them and nail them together like the picture. The flukes can be cut from thin boards like plywood scraps and stuff.

2. **CANNONS** Try and find some short lengths of old stove pipe or soil-pipe — or some big cardboard tubes. Remember, you can make a roll out of thin cardboard and staple or glue it together. The breech can be made with a tin can lid and an old tennis ball. You can make a great carriage out of boards or a small box. With a big spring or some strips of inner tube you can make it shoot too. Let's see if you can figure that out.

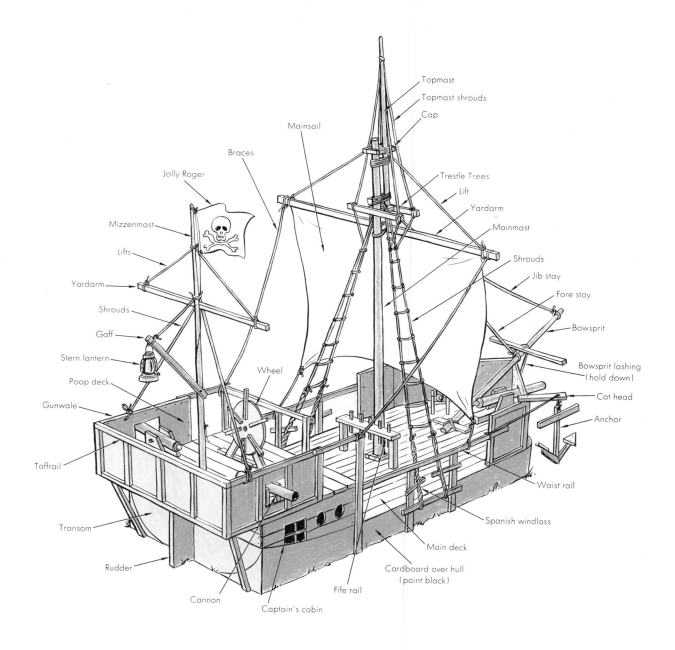

Topmast
Topmast shrouds
Cap
Mainsail
Braces
Trestle Trees
Lift
Yardarm
Jolly Roger
Mainmast
Mizzenmast
Shrouds
Lifts
Jib stay
Fore stay
Yardarm
Shrouds
Bowsprit
Gaff
Bowsprit lashing
(hold down)
Stern lantern
Cat head
Poop deck
Wheel
Anchor
Gunwale
Taffrail
Waist rail
Spanish windlass
Transom
Main deck
Rudder
Cardboard over hull
(paint black)
Cannon
Fife rail
Captain's cabin

3. SHIP'S WHEEL Every ship has to have a wheel for the helmsman, but it is different than most steering wheels. See if you can find a big round lid or cover off a drum or old barrel. Drill a hole in the center for the axle bolt, then nail some sticks on the wheel, so they stick out a little like in the picture. The wheel should be bolted to a stand or box so that it will turn, and you can pretend you are steering the ship.

4. MAST STEP If you can build a frame to fit tightly around the bottom of the mast, you don't need to sink it in the ground because the ropes (shrouds and stays) will hold the mast up. If you want to, you can sink it in the ground a little way for more strength and support.

5. MAINMAST AND TOPMAST FITTING Maybe you have noticed that the masts on a real old time sailing ship are two or more spars spliced or fitted together. Your ship can look just as real if you fit the big lower mast (mainmast) and the little upper mast (topmast) together like it shows in the picture. If you cut some boards and nail them together so they fit tightly around both masts, it will be like the fittings on a real ship. It would be best if you build all of this on the ground, then raise it up.

Notice that the picture shows how the shroud ropes that hold the mast go up and around the mainmast and back down to the deck again. It would be good to drive a nail through the rope into the mast, so it won't slip.

The long boards are called trestle-trees, and, together, they form the crow's nest or main-top. This is where the lookout stands and keeps a weather-eye for whales, islands, treasure galleons or other pirate ships.

6. PIN RAIL or FIFE RAIL This should be built on the deck just behind (abaft) the mast, so that the ropes that pull the sails up and down can be tied (belayed) there. Be sure to use big nails to attach this to the deck because there may be quite a bit of pull from the weight of the sail and yard. The ropes that lead from this rail should go up through pulleys (blocks) then out to the ends of the yards, like it shows in the picture.

7. SHROUD TIGHTENING You will want to have the shroud ropes and stay ropes real tight so that the mast will not wobble. How about making rope ladders on the shrouds too, so you can climb up in the crow's nest? If you can tie a couple of good knots, this is real easy. Just tie a loop knot at the bottom end of each shroud rope, then put a double rope through the loop and tie it to a board nailed to the side of the ship. If you twist the double rope with a board, then brace the board against one of the rail posts, the rigging will be real tight. Be sure to do this with the front and back (fore and aft) stays too. If you want to learn more about how a ship is built and rigged, and about the names of ropes and things, buy a book about ships or check one out at the library.

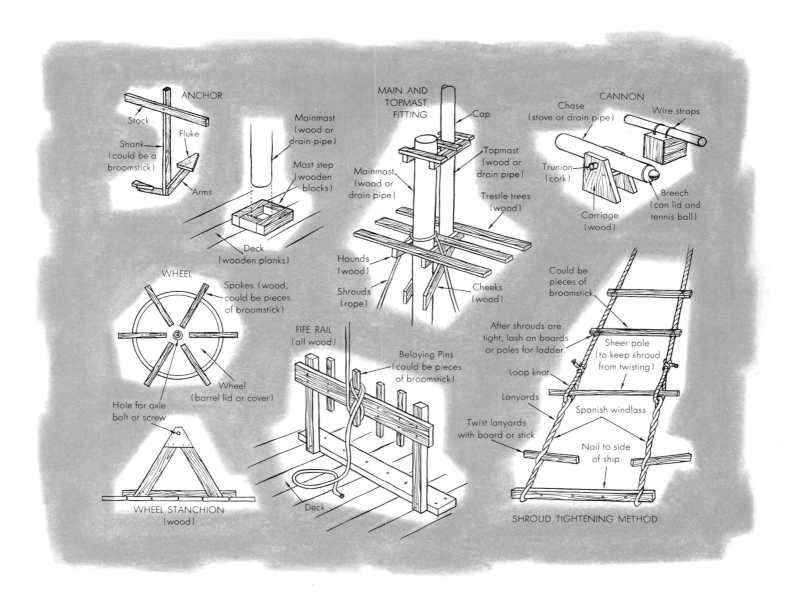

Submarine

Not only does this working submarine look real enough to fool somebody, but it has a set of diving planes so you can make it dive. Make your sub of wood and make sure it will float like a paddleboard or surfboard. Attach floats to your sub so it will always rise quickly and remain buoyant. By ducking under the side and coming up inside the conning tower, it will seem like you are a real submarine captain. You should always run your submarine in shallow water, then by walking on the bottom, you can push the submarine to make it go. By looking through the portholes and periscope, you can see where you're going.

First you'll need two long pieces of wood. They shouldn't be too thick or heavy because they have to bend together at the ends. Once you have bent the long side boards in the shape you want, then nail planks crossways over the top, but leave the planks out where your head and shoulders come through into the conning tower. Next, attach two or more floats. You might try old life preservers or something like them.

A medium-sized box would make a good conning tower, and you need a non-locking escape hatch on top with leather hinges. The conning tower should be nailed firmly to the deck of the submarine. You can make a push bar out of a piece of broomstick, and it can be nailed to the underside of the submarine below the conning tower. By cutting the portholes and opening for the periscope, you will learn how to use a keyhole saw. Study the picture so you can make a good periscope with two mirrors. You may have to build the periscope box out of thin boards.

You can make the diving planes work by using a broomstick or doweling across each end of the submarine through holes in the side boards. The planes can be flat boards nailed to the underside of the dowels or broomsticks like in the picture. With a long stick between each set of diving planes, you can work out a lever device that will make the planes go up or down.

To make the submarine dive, push it as fast as you can then quickly pull the lever back, pointing the diving planes down. At the same time, put your weight on the handlebar to help submerge. Be sure air stays in the conning tower and keeps the water out so you can breath. Also, adjust the floats so the submarine stays under for just a few seconds. Always have an adult test your sub to make sure it floats, surfaces from dives and is completely safe before using it. Of course you should know how to swim, then you'll have a lot of fun pushing your sub around and sighting torpedo targets through the periscope.

14

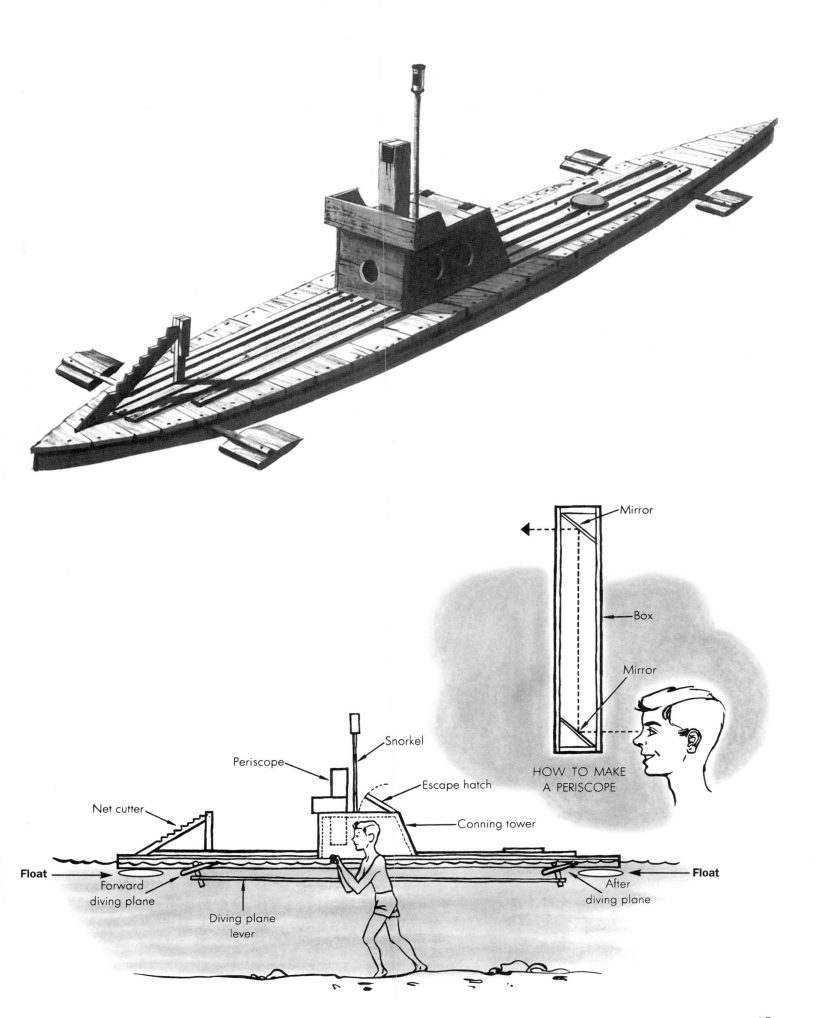

Mirror

Box

Mirror

HOW TO MAKE
A PERISCOPE

Net cutter

Periscope

Snorkel

Escape hatch

Conning tower

Float

Forward
diving plane

Diving plane
lever

After
diving plane

Float

Helicopter

When you crank the rotor blades and work the controls, this whirlybird will seem like it's actually flying — and it's not hard to build either.

First you'll need a big box, then a bunch of long thin battens, like your parents would use to make a rose trellis. Long laths are good too. For the rotor blades you need some thicker wood, or maybe two or three battens laid together flat and nailed with a short cross piece. If you study the picture carefully, you can see the sizes of wood you should use. For instance, some two-by-four pieces would be good for the wheel axles and the center of the rotor blade where you attach the crank. The easiest way to make the rotor blade crank is to find or buy three lengths of one-half inch pipe, two elbow joints and a flange. If you should want to buy some pipe in a hardware store, it would not cost much. Be sure to have a big washer under the flange with lots of grease or oil on it so the rotor blades will turn easily.

The tail propeller (torque prop) can be made with a stick of wood and some plywood or cardboard blades like it shows in the small picture on the next page. You can make it so the wind will make it go around, or if you think you can figure how it works, you could connect the rotor blades and the tail prop with a rope belt. Then the tail propeller will work when you crank the big rotor prop. A piece of inner tube tied in the rope belt will keep it tight.

By studying the pictures, maybe you could make a good joy stick and a cool control panel out of things you can find. Remember too, every helicopter has a hoist rope for raising and lowering supplies and rescuing people in distress!

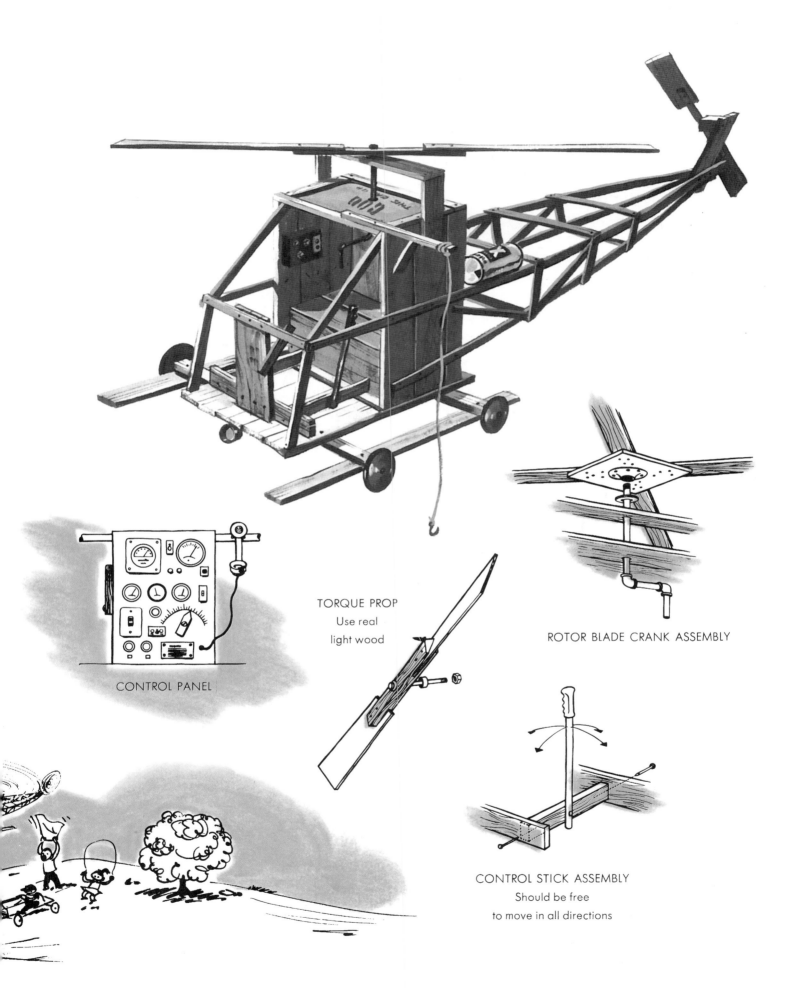

CONTROL PANEL

TORQUE PROP
Use real
light wood

ROTOR BLADE CRANK ASSEMBLY

CONTROL STICK ASSEMBLY
Should be free
to move in all directions

17

Navy Cruiser

a working world class peacekeeper

"Now hear this — all hands to stations, enemy ship bearing 230 degrees, range, three miles, all starboard batteries, open fire!" These are just some of the orders you can shout to your crack crew of sailors and gunners aboard this big powerful cruiser.

Careful study of the picture will show that your ship can be made out of wooden boxes and old boards, and maybe some stovepipe, old drainpipe or large cardboard tubes for guns and smokestacks and things.

If you could get some friends to help and start a real naval shipyard you could have it done in no time. The only tools you'll need are a hammer and a good sharp saw. A drill (brace and bit) and a keyhole saw would be handy for cutting in the doors, hatches and portholes. Remember that if you pile the boxes up to make the bridge and pilot house, they should be nailed together real strong, so they will hold your weight.

The smaller drawings on the next page will show you how to make a real gun turret that will turn from one side of the ship to the other. The big guns sticking out of the front of the turret should be fixed so that they will go up and down.

You can make great ack ack (anti-aircraft) guns, too, as it shows in one of the little drawings. A speaking tube is fun too, so the captain can give orders to the gunners and the men in the engine room. If you make a mast and yardarm like it shows in the picture, you can fly different signal flags like on a real battleship.

The depth charge racks should be made so that the depth charges will roll off the rack one at a time. The depth charges can be made from large cans or ice-cream cartons. These are for sinking submarines by exploding under the water, but it's fun to pretend you are on a real hunt for enemy submarines. It would be fun to put some wheels on the submarine shown on page 15 then you could have a real sea battle!

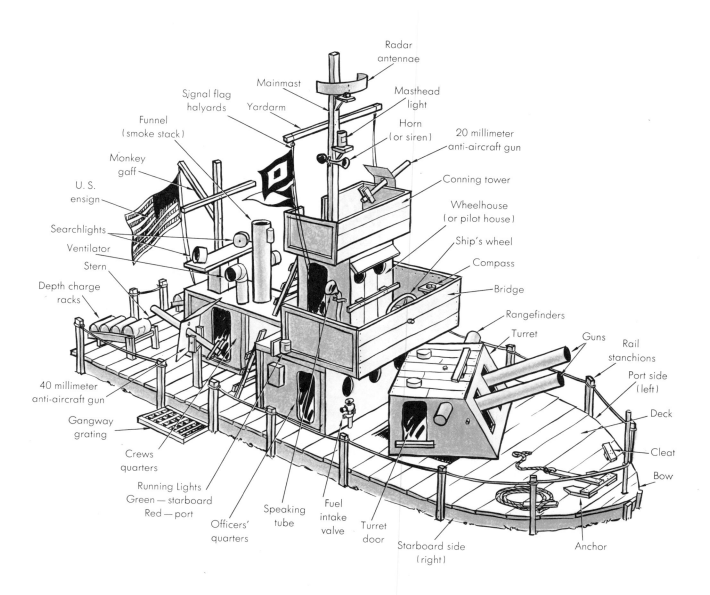

Radar antennae

Mainmast

Signal flag halyards

Yardarm

Masthead light

Funnel (smoke stack)

Horn (or siren)

20 millimeter anti-aircraft gun

Monkey gaff

U. S. ensign

Conning tower

Searchlights

Wheelhouse (or pilot house)

Ventilator

Ship's wheel

Stern

Compass

Depth charge racks

Bridge

Rangefinders

Turret

Guns

Rail stanchions

Port side (left)

40 millimeter anti-aircraft gun

Deck

Gangway grating

Cleat

Crews quarters

Bow

Running Lights
Green — starboard
Red — port

Officers' quarters

Speaking tube

Fuel intake valve

Turret door

Starboard side (right)

Anchor

SEAMAN   **ADMIRAL**   **RADIOMAN**   **GUNNER**

SPEAKING TUBE
To engine room or turret

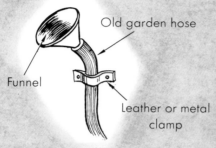

Old garden hose

Funnel

Leather or metal clamp

RANGE FINDER
Tin can or oatmeal box.

CASTER

CASTER
(runs on deck)

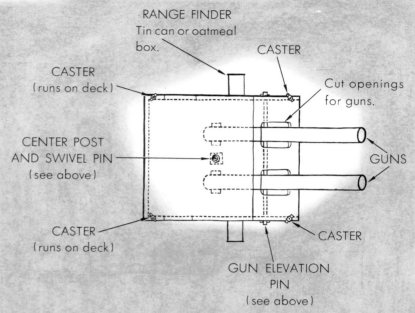

Cut openings for guns.

CENTER POST AND SWIVEL PIN
(see above)

GUNS

CASTER
(runs on deck)

CASTER

GUN ELEVATION PIN
(see above)

40 MM ANTI-AIRCRAFT GUN
(pom-pom gun)

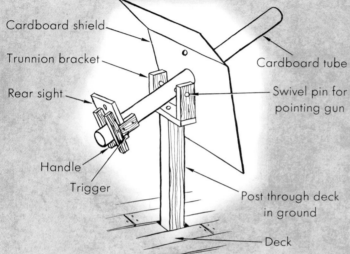

Cardboard shield

Trunnion bracket

Rear sight

Cardboard tube

Swivel pin for pointing gun

Handle

Trigger

Post through deck in ground

Deck

DEPTH CHARGES AND RACK

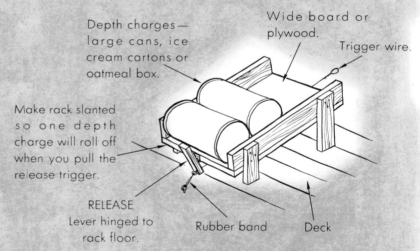

Depth charges—large cans, ice cream cartons or oatmeal box.

Wide board or plywood.

Trigger wire.

Make rack slanted so one depth charge will roll off when you pull the release trigger.

RELEASE
Lever hinged to rack floor.

Rubber band

Deck

GUNS can be made out of old stovepipe or drainpipe—or—cardboard tubes such as rug cores or newspaper roll covers.

ANCHOR

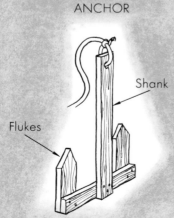

Shank

Flukes

CENTER POST PIN
Use large lag screw or big nail through top of turret, through washer and into top of post.

VENTILATOR
Nail tin can upside down.

TURRET DOOR
Both sides.

GUN ELEVATOR PIN
Long pin (broomstick or pipe) through guns and sides of turret.

TURRET

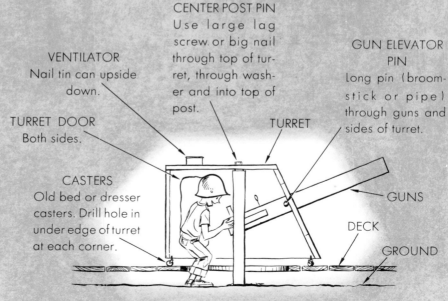

CASTERS
Old bed or dresser casters. Drill hole in under edge of turret at each corner.

GUNS

DECK

GROUND

Sailmobile

It's fun to build and even a lot more fun to sail. Doesn't take much lumber or things either. Just a long wide board (or two boards), a box for a seat, a two-by-four axle for the front wheels, some old tricycle wheels and some poles and cloth for the mast and sails.

If you leave the forks on the front tricycle (or small bicycle) wheel and turn it backwards, it makes a perfect rudder wheel for your sailmobile. The steering tiller can be made from some old pipe or metal tubing. The other two tricycle wheels that are smaller, will work good for the front wheels. Wagon wheels are good too, but not as light as tricycle wheels. You might remember to keep everything as light as you can because the sailmobile will move easier when the wind blows on the sail.

Make sure the long wide board is thick enough so you won't "bottom out" when you hit a bump. Notice that the box for the seat is real wide. That is so you can move your weight over to balance the push of the wind. If there is a pretty good breeze, two can sit in the sailmobile seat.

The mast, boom and gaff can be made out of square sticks or round poles, but not pipe, because we want to keep everything light. An old sheet or some light canvas can be cut to make a great sail.

The sailmobile will always run good on a smooth road or field when the wind is behind and pushing you. If you want to learn how to make it sail in other directions, you might get a book on sailing.

If you live near a lake or a river, and it's wintertime, you could use some old sled runners or ice skates and make a good ice boat.

But never go on the ice unless it's safe and you've received permission from your parents or supervising adult. Remember, safety first!

Western Buildings

Wouldn't it be fun to build a whole town? If you round up your neighborhood friends to look for lots of big boxes, boards, nails, paint and lanterns, you could make a real western town! Your stagecoach and covered wagon could come rumbling through to pick up passengers and supplies. Or, you could make one of the buildings a train station if you wanted to make a train too.

Maybe you would want to make just one building for a clubhouse or something. How big you make the buildings doesn't really matter, just so you can get inside them and spy out through the windows when the gunslingers shoot it out. In the sheriff's office, you could make a jail to put the outlaws in. You could use some old broomsticks or mop handles for bars.

If a lady came to town in the stagecoach, she would probably want to stay at the hotel. You should fix this up real fancy with curtains and everything. You could even use this town for an action movie set and make your own westerns with a video camera.

There are lots of ways to make a clubhouse or buildings, but maybe if you study the picture, you can get some good ideas. It's a lot of fun to try and make them look like real western buildings or an old desert ghost town!

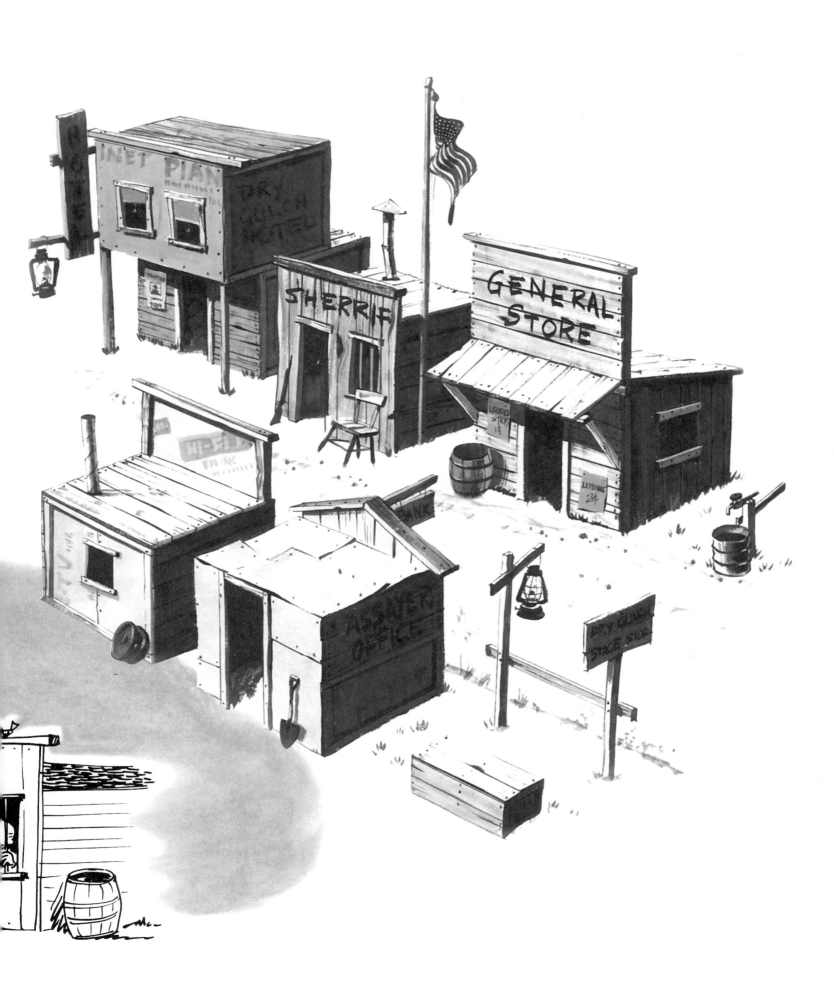

Hot Rod Car
or Soap Box Derby Racer

Boy, this is a real neat car and with real brakes too! You should be pretty handy with a saw and a hammer before you tackle this one unless you can get your parents or a friend to help. This racer can be officially entered in a soap box derby, or you can have lots of fun just coasting down the hills in your neighborhood or local park.

A long, wide plank or two planks nailed together make the best frame or chassis. Two lengths of two-by-four make the best axle bars. Then you'll need some iron bar stock for axles, but be sure that they fit the wheels that you have selected. The iron axle rods should be attached to the wooden axle bars with U bolts, not bent nails! The rear axle bar should be bolted to the chassis with two or three bolts. Because the front axle bar has to turn, you should use only one large bolt in the center.

After your axles and wheels are on, you might give it a road test to see if everything is working good. Then build up the hood and seat like the picture. If you go to an automobile wrecking yard, you can get an old steering wheel and shaft. You may have to cut the end of the iron shaft off to make it fit your car, but this is easy with a hacksaw because the shaft is hollow like a pipe. When you have the wheel and shaft in place, wind some rope around the shaft and lead each end through a pulley and tie it to the ends of the front axle bar. If you tie a clove hitch knot in the middle of the winds, it will keep the steering rope from slipping.

The brakes are real easy to make, but you'd better study the picture first. Maybe this is where parents can help best, but it would be fun to try yourself.

There are a lot of different ways to make a good soap box hot rod, and no matter how you build it or what it looks like, you and your friends will have real exciting fun.

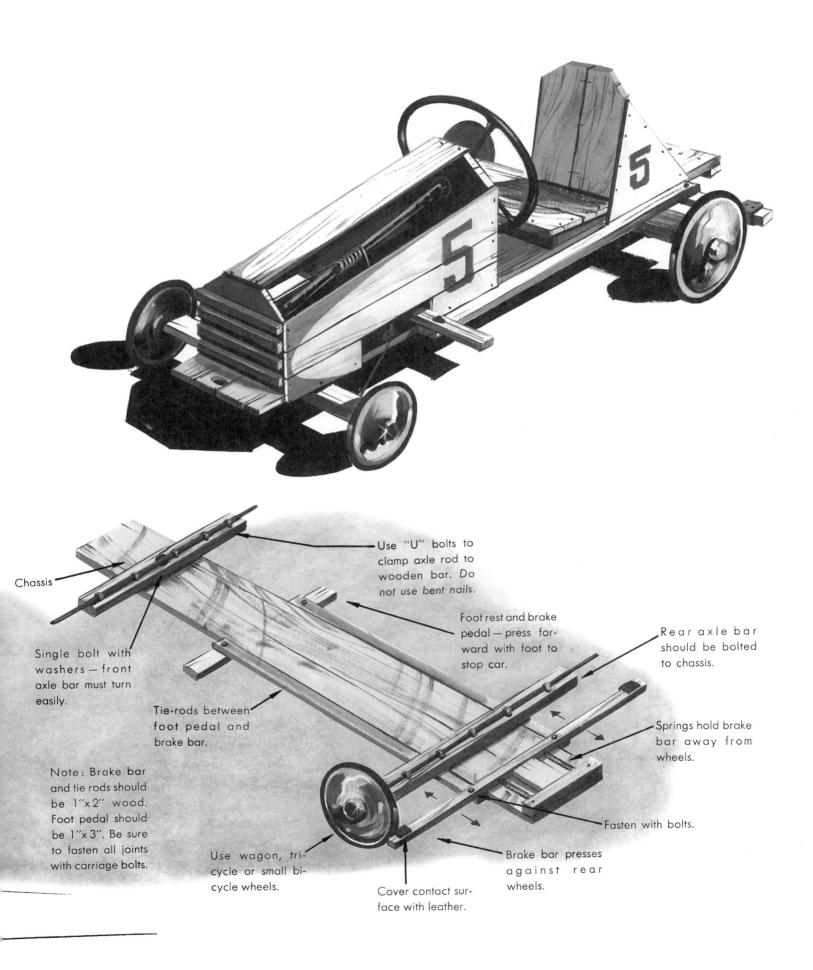

Chassis

Use "U" bolts to clamp axle rod to wooden bar. *Do not use bent nails.*

Foot rest and brake pedal — press forward with foot to stop car.

Rear axle bar should be bolted to chassis.

Single bolt with washers — front axle bar must turn easily.

Tie-rods between foot pedal and brake bar.

Springs hold brake bar away from wheels.

Note: Brake bar and tie rods should be 1"x 2" wood. Foot pedal should be 1"x 3". Be sure to fasten all joints with carriage bolts.

Use wagon, tricycle or small bicycle wheels.

Fasten with bolts.

Brake bar presses against rear wheels.

Cover contact surface with leather.

Stagecoach

We need to have a stagecoach to carry gold and passengers between the frontier and the fort. You could call it The Butterfield Stage just like the real stages that traveled all over the Western deserts and mountains.

The Butterfield Overland Mail Stagecoach service began in 1858 and ran between St. Louis, MO and San Francisco, CA. It was a rugged, unpleasant trip, but if you were in St. Louis and had business in San Francisco, the Butterfield Line would get you there in only 23 days!

Remember that the driver sits on the right and the man who "rides shotgun" should sit on the left. He should carry a big shotgun or rifle to defend against outlaws and bandits. After the passengers have paid their fare, they can ride inside the coach to the place they want to go. Baggage, freight and gold shipments are put on top of the stagecoach or on the luggage rack in back.

Sometimes, to make a good stagecoach, you will have to use more tools besides a hammer and saw. You will need a big box or some lumber and four wheels. Real old fashion wagon wheels are the very best, but today they are not easy to find. The next best thing would be some bicycle wheels because they are bigger and will make your stagecoach easier to pull. To see the best way to attach the wheels, look back to the picture of the soap box car on page 27. You can make the brake work like it shows on the soap box car too.

The big picture shows how you might make a real-looking stagecoach, but if you would rather, you could make a smaller one on top of your wagon. This could be made like the covered wagon on page 5 except that you would put a flat roof over the box instead of the bent sticks and cloth. A little door cut in the side of the box would look more real, and the passengers could get in and out easier.

28

One stage service ran three times a week between San Francisco and San Jose, California. The trip was about 50 miles and took nine hours one way. The coaches held eight passengers (or in a pinch, ten), and the fare per passenger was $32 or two ounces of gold. In a storm, the journey took as long as 16 hours, and the passengers often had to get out in mud axle-deep and help push! Later fares were lowered to $16 and then to $10.

Rocket Ship

with Radar Blockhouse

Rocket ready for blast off, sir! Countdown 10, 9, 8, 7, 6, 5, 4, 3, 2, 1, fire! With a roaring blast of flame, your space rocket begins to lift, slow at first, then faster and faster, up and up through the troposphere, ionosphere, then the BREAKTHROUGH into outer space! The blockhouse control has you on its radar screen. The beeps from your nose cone are being transmitted back to earth. You are off in the vast mysterious void of space!

Talk about fun? This is the greatest! All you need is some old 50-gallon drums for the rockets, about three wooden boxes and some lumber, cardboard and cloth. You'll want to look for some old instruments, dials and switches too. Then you can fix up the control room like a real space ship.

First, the rocket tubes (barrels or drums) go on the ground. It might help to tie them together with a rope for stability. Support stakes driven into the ground is another way to secure them. Then, pile about three big boxes on top of the drums and nail them together. The top box should be your control room. Cut an access door and some portholes (viewplates) in the sides. This is to see where you're going and also to watch the ground disappear when you blast off.

Some strong boards braced against the middle box can be covered to look like fins and will help support the boxes too. Some large cans or round cartons can be fastened to the sides for booster rockets. On the top box, you can make a nose cone by tying four sticks together. Then, cover them with cardboard or some cloth. Some tinker-toy sticks and balls would make good "beep" antennae. If you have a toy telephone set, you could talk from the rocket control room to the blockhouse and give the blast off orders to the radar control staff.

Remember, when you land on a planet or return back to earth, you should reverse the ship and land stern first, using your rocket blast to cushion the landing!

31

Rocket Missile Launcher

Really shoots with strips of old inner tube for launching sling

You just can't have an army without a rocket launcher! And you can make it really shoot, too, just like a big slingshot or rubberband gun. If you want to move your rocket launcher to different places, you should build it on some wheels like in the picture. Of course, it will work just as good if you first build it on the ground, but be sure and aim it toward a vacant lot or a big empty space!

You'll need some long straight boards for this one. First, you should make the lower frame or carriage of two by fours. The launching track can be made with a long board about six inches wide. To keep the rocket going straight on the launching track, you can nail a long strip of wood on each side. You might need some help from a grownup to make the elevation levers work, but if you study the picture, it's really not hard. If you would rather not make the levers, you could just nail a couple of boards to hold up the launching track.

To make the missile really shoot, you need to find an old tire inner tube, then cut the rubber in long strips and tie the ends together forming a great big rubber band. Now nail the rubber sling to the very end of the launching track, and then pull it way back and slip the band over the trigger bar. It might take two of you to stretch the rubber real tight.

The trigger bar can be one or two sticks nailed to the side of the launching track near the bottom. These should be propped up with another stick that is nailed to the lower frame. By stepping on the prop stick, the trigger bar will let go of the rubber, and your rocket missile will really take off. Remember, the tighter you pull the rubber sling, the farther your rocket will go.

The smaller drawing shows how to make a good rocket missile out of a mailing tube and some cardboard or balsa wood. Be sure to keep the rocket real light so the launcher can shoot it clear across your yard or an empty lot.

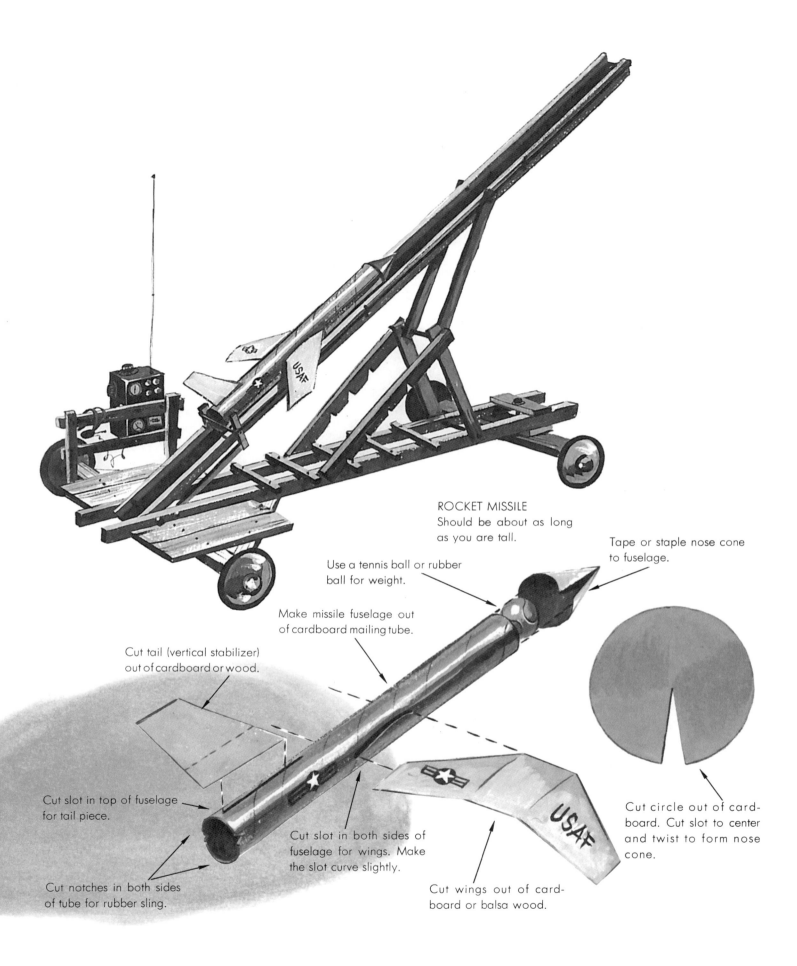

ROCKET MISSILE
Should be about as long as you are tall.

Tape or staple nose cone to fuselage.

Use a tennis ball or rubber ball for weight.

Make missile fuselage out of cardboard mailing tube.

Cut tail (vertical stabilizer) out of cardboard or wood.

Cut slot in top of fuselage for tail piece.

Cut notches in both sides of tube for rubber sling.

Cut slot in both sides of fuselage for wings. Make the slot curve slightly.

Cut wings out of cardboard or balsa wood.

Cut circle out of cardboard. Cut slot to center and twist to form nose cone.

Castle

Think of the fun you'd have with a real castle and a drawbridge that lowers down over the moat! You could dress up like knights with swords and shields, and then rescue the princess that is being held prisoner in the castle tower. You and a neighbor girl could be the king and queen, or maybe, it could be another boy and girl, or you could take turns. You would have to make a nice crown for the king and queen, and they should have a throne in the castle too. You might think of some ways to make a suit of armor out of cardboard and old mailing tubes.

Remember, a knight was always very polite to ladies and always helped them whenever he could. In the days of knights and castles, this was called chivalry.

To build a good castle you'd probably need some help from some of your friends. The towers can be made out of large wooden boxes, or you can build them up with boards. The bottom box of the tower would be the dungeon. The castle walls could be made out of the large bicycle cartons that you can get from a bicycle shop or department store. These big sheets of cardboard can be nailed to posts and boxes, and then you can paint them to look like big stones or rocks. Around the sides of the towers you should nail some short boards to look like battlements. These are the slots in the walls and towers of all real castles.

A real storybook castle would have flags and streamers flying from all the towers. The flags, capes and robes could be made out of old pieces of cloth or even crepe paper. These would be fun things to make with your own designs. Maybe your parents would help with some of the decorations and costumes.

Remember, a castle should have a moat! That's a ditch or a trough of water clear around the castle so the attacking army can't get close to the walls. The drawbridge at the castle gate should go across the moat so the knights and ladies and carriages can go in and out. See if you can figure out a good way to make the drawbridge go up and down with ropes and pulleys. You can make good pulley wheels out of old tricycle or wagon wheels. If you take the rubber tires off the wheels, you will see how the rope can ride over the metal rim.

You might get some good ideas for castles from other books. There are lots of wonderful stories about castles, dungeons and knights in your local library.

Cable Car

Have you ever had a ride in a cable car? This is great fun! You could make it go across a corner of your yard or a small stream. Maybe the older kids in your family or around the neighborhood could help. Of course when they help, they'll want to play with it too.

You probably can get a good wooden box and a few boards, but first you should get lots of rope and two pulleys. The rope should be about as thick as a man's thumb, or larger (3/4 inch in diameter). Be sure the box and the hanging boards are fastened together well with strong nails, screws or bolts.

The easiest place to swing the cable car is in between two large trees or big poles like telephone poles or strong fence posts. You can stretch the rope or wire and tighten it by twisting two strands of rope with a stick. This is called a Spanish Windlass.

When you don't have trees or large poles, you can make a shear-legs out of some two-by-fours or straight tree limbs. If you look closely at the picture on the next page, it will show you how to stretch the wire over the shear legs and down to an anchor buried pretty deep in the ground. Then your cable car can hang from two pulleys that ride along the tight wire. You can pull yourself along with a smaller rope attached to the anchor at each end.

Maybe your dad, older brothers or uncles would like to know a secret: A cable car above a stream or small river is a great place to fish from.

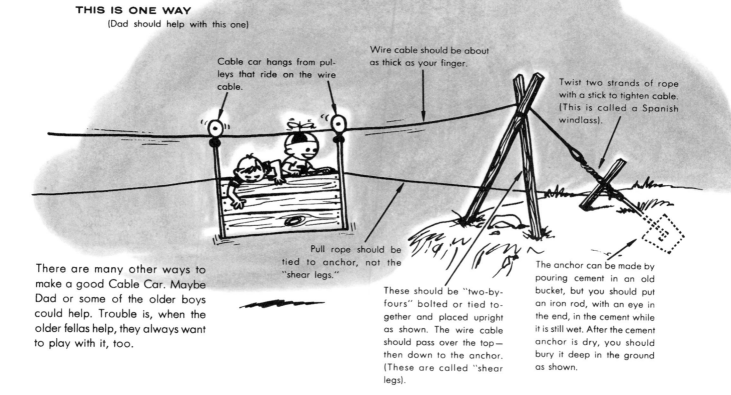

THIS IS ONE WAY
(Dad should help with this one)

Cable car hangs from pulleys that ride on the wire cable.

Wire cable should be about as thick as your finger.

Twist two strands of rope with a stick to tighten cable. (This is called a Spanish windlass).

Pull rope should be tied to anchor, not the "shear legs."

There are many other ways to make a good Cable Car. Maybe Dad or some of the older boys could help. Trouble is, when the older fellas help, they always want to play with it, too.

These should be "two-by-fours" bolted or tied together and placed upright as shown. The wire cable should pass over the top — then down to the anchor. (These are called "shear legs).

The anchor can be made by pouring cement in an old bucket, but you should put an iron rod, with an eye in the end, in the cement while it is still wet. After the cement anchor is dry, you should bury it deep in the ground as shown.

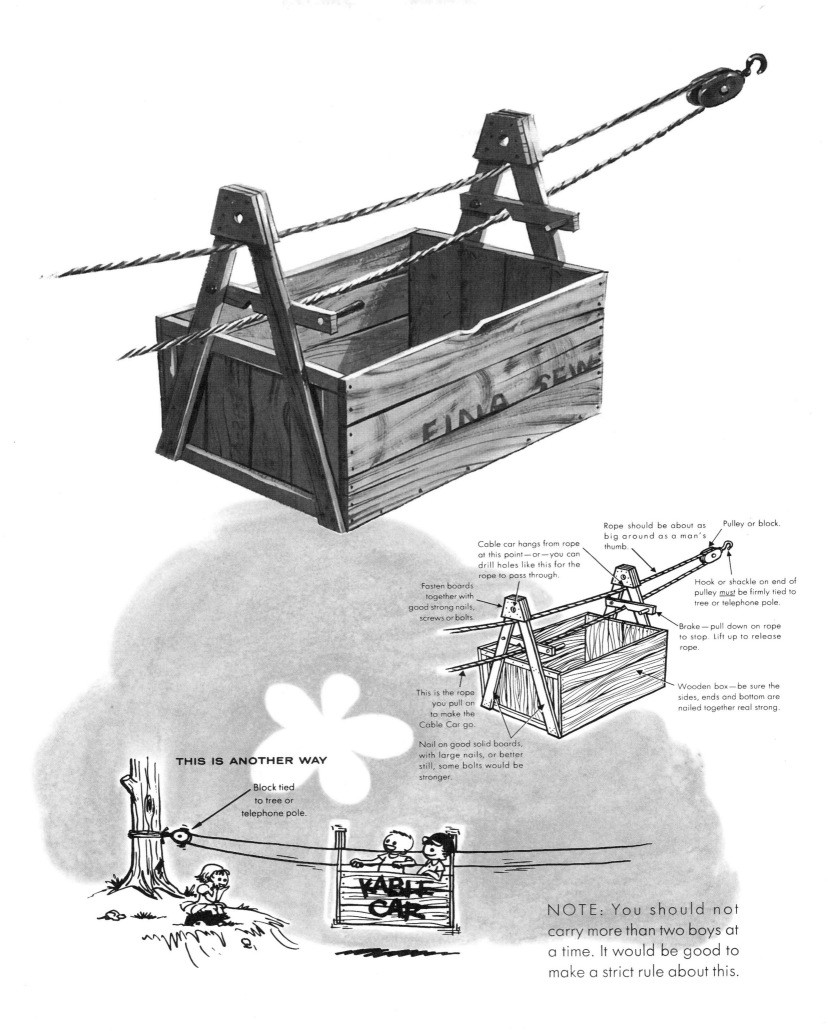

Rope should be about as big around as a man's thumb.

Pulley or block.

Cable car hangs from rope at this point—or—you can drill holes like this for the rope to pass through.

Hook or shackle on end of pulley *must* be firmly tied to tree or telephone pole.

Fasten boards together with good strong nails, screws or bolts.

Brake—pull down on rope to stop. Lift up to release rope.

This is the rope you pull on to make the Cable Car go.

Wooden box—be sure the sides, ends and bottom are nailed together real strong.

Nail on good solid boards, with large nails, or better still, some bolts would be stronger.

THIS IS ANOTHER WAY

Block tied to tree or telephone pole.

KABLE CAR

NOTE: You should not carry more than two boys at a time. It would be good to make a strict rule about this.

Army Tent

A real easy thing to make is a tent. There are many kinds of tents you could make with some old canvas, or even some old sheets or blankets. An army tent is the most fun because your neighborhood friends could help build it and use it. The tent could probably be the general's headquarters, and it could have a radio and telephone, and it should have a flagpole too. Maybe a cannon would be a good thing to build, so the headquarters can be protected against the enemy.

If you have a cot, maybe your parents would let you sleep in the tent all night. Lots of soldiers just sleep on the ground in a sleeping bag or blanket roll, but it's best to do this in the summertime.

Remember, good soldiers always keep their quarters neat and clean. Sometimes the general holds inspection just to see that everything is according to army regulations.

Native American Tepee

You have probably read some books in school about Native Americans, or have seen stories of them on television or in the movies. Native Americans lived in the land before settlers came. They knew all about living off the land and could do many wonderful things.

The tepee was like a tent that Native Americans lived in. It was made by stacking several long poles together like it shows in the picture. Originally, these poles were covered with buffalo skins. Of course, you might have some trouble finding a buffalo around today! It would be best to cover your tepee with some old canvas or cloth, then you can paint some tribal symbols all around the sides. Tepees are fun to hold club meetings in, or to sleep overnight in if it's all right with your parents. Maybe if you could get everyone in the neighborhood together you could build some other tepees and have a village. You might think of a lot of Native American articles to make, such as ceremonial drums, feather bonnets, tomahawks and peace pipes.

If you are interested in Native American artifacts find a book about this subject at the library. By studying the pictures, you can figure out how to make all sorts of native crafts and costumes out of sticks and cloth and cardboard and paper.

HOW TO ORDER THIS BOOK ←- - - - - -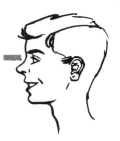

Also, get on our mailing list for free by filling out the form below!

BY PHONE

Call Toll Free!
1-800-205-8254
Visa
MasterCard
American Express

BY COMPUTER

On-line orders!
Website: http://www.bookzone.com/
Find us in the Children's Aisle or
search by book title, author,
publisher or ISBN# 0-9651275-6-7

BY MAIL

Postal orders!
Infotainment
P.O. Box 1244
Parker, CO., 80134-1244

Even if you're not ordering, send in your name and address on this form to get on our mailing list free of charge. We'll keep you informed about *"Backyard" Things* building contests, new book releases and other excitement from Infotainment.

━ ORDER FORM / MAILING LIST ━

Quanity	Title	Price Each	Total
	"Backyard" Things That Are Fun To Build!	$12.95	

ADD POSTAGE
(Surface shipping may take three to four weeks)

$2.50 for 1st book
.50 for each additional book
Air Mail: $3.50 per book

POSTAGE

ADD
Total Price
& Postage
from above

Quanity discounts available to volume buyers (25 or more copies): write to Infotainment for more information.

ORDER TOTAL

☐ **YES!** Put me on your mailing list for free!

Send check or money order to:
Infotainment
P.O. Box 1244
Parker, CO., 80134-1244

Company name:
_____

Name:
_____

Address:
_____

City: _____ State: _____ Zip: _____

Telephone: ( )
_____

clip or copy